GALWAY

GALWAY

City of Heritage

Pat Dargan

EASTWOOD BOOKS

First published 2024 by Eastwood Books
Dublin, Ireland
www.eastwoodbooks.com
www.wordwellbooks.com

1

Eastwood Books is an imprint of the Wordwell Group.

The Wordwell Group is a member of Publishing Ireland,
the Irish Publishers' Association.

Eastwood Books
The Wordwell Group
Unit 9, 78 Furze Road
Sandyford
Dublin, Ireland

ISBN: 978-1-913934-58-3 (Trade Paperback)

British Library Cataloguing in Publication Data.
A catalogue record for this book is available from the National Library of Ireland and
the British Library.

Typesetting and design by the Wordwell Group
Copyediting by Emer Condit
Printed in Ireland by Sprint Print, Dublin

Contents

Previous published works by the author

Exploring Georgian Dublin, 2008
Exploring Ireland's Historic Towns, 2010
Exploring Irish Castles, 2011
Exploring Celtic Ireland, 2011
Exploring Georgian Limerick, 2012
Georgian Bath, 2012
Georgian London – the West End, 2012
The Georgian Town House, 2013
Edinburgh New Town, co-authored by Carley, Dalziel and Laird, 2015
Dublin in 50 Buildings, 2017
Bath in 50 Buildings, 2018
Dublin Pubs, 2018
Limerick in 50 Buildings, 2019
Kilkenny – City of Heritage, 2020
Whitehaven in 50 Buildings, 2021
Wexford: Town of Heritage, 2023
Farnham in 50 Buildings, 2023

List of Buildings

1. St Nicholas's Church, Churchyard Street–Lombard Street
2. Town wall, Eyre Square Centre
3. Head of the Wall Bastion, Spanish Parade
4. Blake tower-house, Quay Street
5. Lynch tower-house, Shop Street
6. Medieval house, Quay Street
7. Medieval house, Kirwan's Lane
8. Corner house, Spanish Parade
9. Medieval house front, Eyre Square
10. Lynch Memorial Wall, Lombard Street
11. Former corner house, Abbeygate Street
12. Martin house, Cross Street/Quay Street
13. Mayoral house, St Augustine Street
14. House, William Street
15. Joyce house, Church Lane
16. Former warehouse, Kirwan's Lane
17. Former warehouse, St Augustine Street
18. Joyce town house, St Augustine Street
19. Rendered town house, Eyre Street
20. End-of-terrace house, Eyre Square
21. Bank of Ireland building, Eyre Square
22. Former courthouse, Courthouse Square
23. Former town hall, Courthouse Square
24. Shop, Williamsgate Street
25. Former warehouse, Merchant's Road
26. Semi-detached town house, Eyre Square
27. Augustinian priory, St Augustine Street

28. United Methodist and Presbyterian church, Queen Street
29. Terraced town house, Spanish Parade
30. Galway railway station, Station Road
31. Hibernian House, Eyre Square
32. Franciscan church, St Francis Street
33. Hotel, Eyre Square
34. Former market house, Eyre Square
35. Town house, Dock Road
36. Former department store, William Street/Eglinton Street
37. Colonial Building, Williamsgate Street/Eglinton Street
38. Two-storey terraced house, St Francis Street
39. Former Catholic cathedral, Middle Street
40. Augustinian church, Middle Street
41. Convent of Mercy church, Newtownsmith
42. Former corner house, Shop Street/Churchyard Street
43. Corner retail store, William Street/Abbeygate Street
44. Office building, Merchant's Road
45. Galway Cathedral, University Road

Opposite page: Diagrammatic map of the historic core of Galway with the position of the selected buildings indicated.

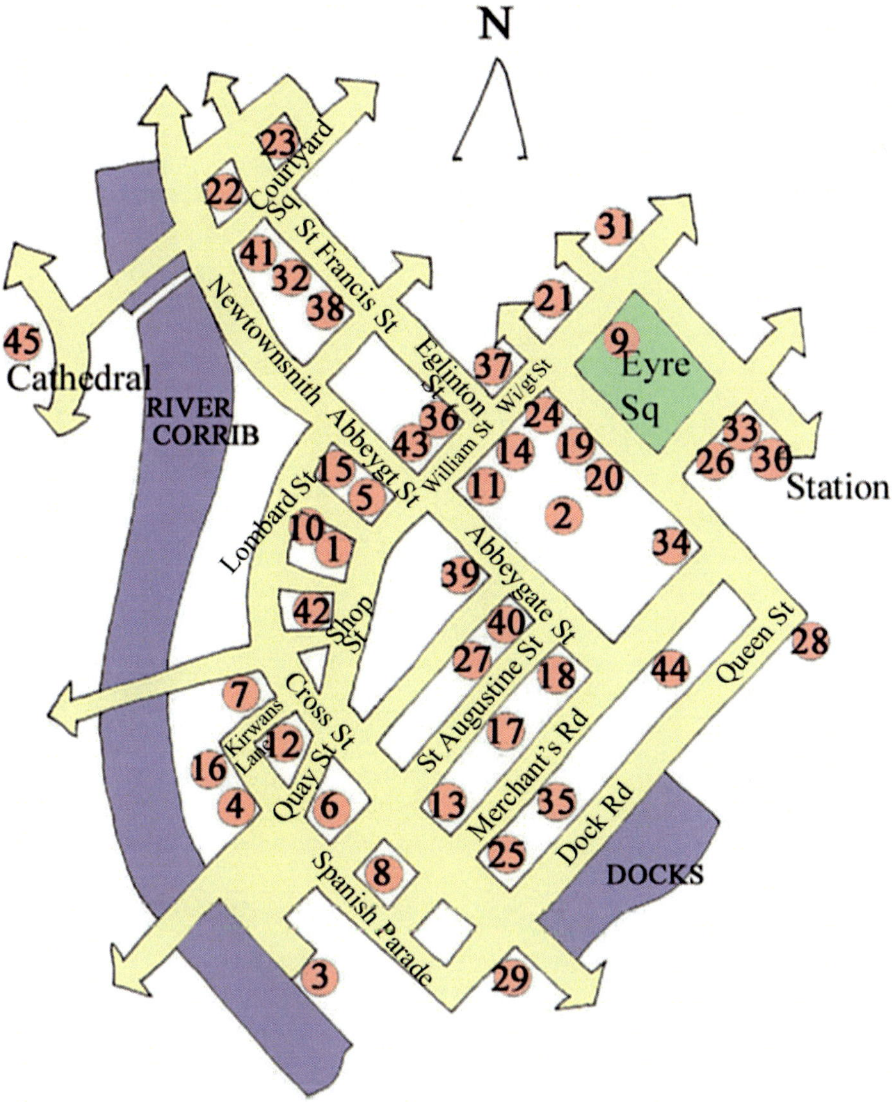
N
Courtyard Sq
St Francis St
Newtownsnith
Eglinton St
Wi/gt St
William St
Abbeygt St
Lombard St
Shop St
Abbeygate St
St Augustine St
Merchant's Rd
Cross St
Kirwans Lane
Quay St
Spanish Parade
Dock Rd
Queen St
Eyre Sq
Station
Cathedral
RIVER CORRIB
DOCKS
1 2 3 4 5 6 7 8 9 10 11 12 13 14 15 16 17 18 19 20 21 22 23 24 25 26 27 28 29 30 31 32 33 34 35 36 37 38 39 40 41 42 43 44 45

Introduction

The city of Galway has a rich body of historic buildings that date from its establishment in the thirteenth century to the present day. The city is positioned on the estuary of the River Corrib where it enters Galway Bay on the west coast of Ireland. It was initially founded by the Norman Richard de Burgo, who chose to build his castle here around 1220, and, despite Gaelic opposition, a Norman urban settlement had became permanently established by 1270. Shortly afterwards, work began on the defence of the settlement by a town wall that enclosed around eleven hectares, and work began on forming riverside quays. Inside the walls the town was laid out in an irregular street grid that included Market Street, Shop Street, Middle Street, St Augustine Street, Abbeygate Street and Cross Street, all lined with closely packed medieval houses, with the parish church of St Nicholas in a central position. A number of religious orders, such as the Augustinians, Franciscans and Dominicans, established houses outside the walls.

For most of the medieval period the city prospered under the influence of fourteen merchant families who successfully traded with European centres such as Portugal and Spain, but it suffered during the English Civil War and the Jacobean wars of the seventeenth century and slipped into commercial decline. The Georgian and Victorian periods of the eighteenth and nineteenth centuries saw renewed growth and the outward expansion of the city, including the laying out of a range of public administration and educational buildings, in both central and suburban locations. In addition, Eyre Square was laid out as a garden square, and extensive harbour facilities were established on the southern rim of the city. The growth of the city's fabric was particularly notable during the nineteenth century, when, in addition to commercial and residential growth, a range of civil and ecclesiastical projects, including churches, courthouse, town hall and railway station, were set in place, particularly inside the line of the medieval wall, between 1800 and 1850—effectively completing the city's historic core.

The great expansion of Galway city took place, however, during the twentieth century, when a network of residential, service, industrial and institutional elements filled the hinterland beyond the historic core as far as suburban Salthill and Renmore. Today the central historic area of Galway houses much of the city's historic architecture, a selection of which are presented in the writer's belief that they represent the most interesting examples of the city's historic buildings. These are presented in the chronological order in which they appeared and can be seen as representing a physical testament of the city's local history.

Medieval Galway

The medieval buildings of Galway date approximately from between 1300 and 1600 and fall into the Gothic phase of architecture witnessed all across Europe during the Middle Ages—an architectural movement that incorporated heavy stone walling, cut-stone pointed-arched door and window openings, buttresses, gabled roofs, towers and military elements. Although few examples of medieval buildings survive in Galway, those that do include St Nicholas's Church, a number of tower-houses and small sections of the town wall.

1. St Nicholas's Collegiate Church, Churchyard Street/Lombard Street, 1320

The Collegiate Church of St Nicholas is a fine example of Irish Gothic architecture. Its foundation dates from 1320, marking it as the oldest medieval building in the city. It stands near the centre of the medieval sector, slotted between Churchyard Street and Lombard Street. The term 'Collegiate' refers to a unique event in 1484, when a college of clergy was appointed by the mayor and corporation of the city to administer the church independently of episcopal control. Following the Reformation in 1532, the administration of the church was assumed by the Church of Ireland. By this period the church had all the characteristic elements of Gothic architecture and it represents the most distinguished historic feature of Galway, reflecting as it does the wealth and ecclesiastical life of the successful medieval city. The Churchyard Street elevation, for example, features heavy stone walling and an arrangement of side porches, steep gables, corner turrets, buttresses, battlemented roof lines, slated roofs, pointed door and window openings, and a tall tower (Fig. 1). The windows vary from slim lancets to wide and elaborate examples of tracery with moulded surrounds and elaborate stained-glass working. The plainer but no less impressive Lombard Street elevation has three pronounced gabled bays, representing the roof line of the nave and side aisles (Fig. 2). Each of the tall Gothic windows has intricate tracery, stained glass and hood-moulding (Fig. 3). The tall, square clock tower positioned over the nave and transept crossing has corner buttresses, battlemented parapets, two clock faces, louvred openings and a tall crowning spire (Fig. 4). Internally the church has a cruciform layout that includes the nave, transepts and side aisles. The nave is separated from the side aisles by a pattern of arched arcades carried on square columns with decorated heads and plain rendered walling overhead. The plain barrel-vaulted roof is plastered except for the south transept, which has timber sheeting and a wooden arched braced roof structure. The interior also has a rich arrangement of burial and memorial wall plaques, including the elaborate sixteenth-century Lynch window and Joyce wall tomb.

Fig. 1—St Nicholas's Church, Churchyard Street, displays many of the characteristic elements of Irish Gothic architecture, including heavy masonry walling and steep gables, as well as Gothic arched windows and doorways.

Fig. 2—The elevations of St Nicholas's Church, with triple gables, incorporating tall Gothic windows and tracery.

Below left: Fig. 3—Gothic gable windows of St Nicholas's Church, with intricate tracery, stained glass and hood-mouldings.

Below right: Fig. 4—The tower of St Nicholas's Church extends above the slated roof, with louvred openings, battlements, gabled clock faces on two sides, and a tall, pointed copper spire.

2. Town walls, Eyre Square Centre, fourteenth century

Galway, like many other towns in medieval Ireland, was enclosed by a defensive wall, which protected an irregular rectangular area of around eleven hectares. Work on the wall began in the thirteenth century, and it was completed in various stages between the thirteenth and seventeenth centuries. During the eighteenth century most of the town walls were removed and today little survives, except for a small section adjacent to the Head of the Wall Bastion (Building 3) and a more extensive section within the Eyre Square Centre shopping complex. Extensive archaeological excavation during the construction of the complex revealed part of the town wall between two fourteenth-century towers, the Penrose (Fig. 5) and Shoemaker towers. The remains of the stone wall and the two D-shaped towers were subsequently rebuilt to their original height and were incorporated into the shopping centre, where they are currently a feature; the wall and towers were covered with a glazed roof, and a narrow open exhibition space was arranged at one side (Fig. 6). As the floor level on either side of the wall differs, a footbridge was built to link the different heights, and at the same time a doorway was opened into the Shoemaker's Tower (Fig. 7).

Fig. 5—Partially rebuilt Penrose Tower and glazed roof, Eyre Square Centre.

Right: Fig. 6—Restored medieval town wall, with exhibition area and tower, Eyre Square Centre.

Below: Fig. 7—New doorway and railings to the medieval Shoemaker's Tower, Eyre Square Centre.

3. Head of the Wall Bastion, Spanish Parade, 1584

An additional element, the Head of the Wall Bastion, was added to the town defences around 1584. Today frequently but mistakenly referred to as the Spanish Arch, this was a stone bastion built by the mayor of Galway, William Martin, in the form of a wide flanking extension to the main town wall that stretched as far as the water's edge to screen and protect the shipping berthed in the medieval harbour (Fig. 8). It was only later, in the eighteenth century, that the arches were inserted at ground level to provide access to the recently developed harbour extension undertaken by the Eyre family. The bastion was originally longer and included four arches but was partially destroyed in 1755 owing to the effects of the tsunami generated by the Lisbon Earthquake. Today the wide rectangular stone structure with its two surviving semicircular archways is a notable landmark feature of medieval Galway, particularly relating to the harbour. Immediately adjoining the tower is a short section of the town wall (Fig. 9), one of the few surviving sections. It has a flat parapet carried on stone corbels and a projecting high-level defensive gallery at one end (Fig. 10).

Fig. 8—The medieval Head of the Wall Bastion on Spanish Parade, with eighteenth-century arches cut through it.

Fig. 9—Medieval town wall at the rear of the Head of the Wall Bastion, with heavy masonry and corbelled parapet.

Fig. 10—Corbelled defensive gallery, Head of the Wall Bastion.

4. The Blake tower-house, Quay Street, 1470

Military defence was also considered an important factor within the town walls, and a number of tower-houses, or small castles, were built to shield their occupants from attack in turbulent times. These tower-houses were usually square, three or four storeys high, with a defended door at ground level, small windows—usually confined to the upper levels—and rooftop battlements. Internally the tower-house generally has a single room and a smaller gallery on each floor level, with a circular staircase in one corner for access. The Blake tower-house is a tall, three-storey stone tower that faces Quay Street. It was built around 1470 and is one of many similar tower-houses that survive in the medieval sector of many Irish towns. It is integrated into the adjoining streetscape and only one face is visible from the street front (Fig. 11). The recently built commercial buildings on either side of the tower are set back slightly, however, and this helps to define the form and character of the tower.

The Blake tower fulfilled a number of functions in its past, including use as a gaol, a store and a restaurant. It was entered by means of a cut-stone archway, although the current wooden door is a recent replacement. Overhead, the structure has a number of windows. The first level has a small central window as well as an unusual carved and decorated corner window (Fig. 12), while the second level has a pair of square windows. The roof line above is shielded by battlements, and a projecting machicolation supported on corbels was intended to control the doorway immediately beneath in the event of an attack (Fig. 13).

Opposite left: Fig. 11—Blake urban tower-house with medieval defences facing onto Quay Street.

Opposite Right: Fig. 12—Ogee corner window of the Blake tower-house.

Above: Fig. 13—Projecting roof-level machicolation of the Blake tower-house, positioned directly above the entrance.

5. Lynch tower-house, Shop Street, 1500

This stone tower-house on the corner of Shop Street and Abbeygate Street was owned by the Lynches, one of the ruling families of Galway. It dates from around 1500 but has undergone considerable changes both internally and externally (Fig. 14). The building was originally five storeys high and its corner position allows its full scale to be appreciated from the street. Internally the number of floors was reduced to four. The original windows were blocked up and replacement Georgian windows were inserted into the masonry at the new floor levels during the nineteenth century. Fortunately, a number of the original mullioned and transomed windows have survived, albeit in a blocked-up state (Fig. 15). Nevertheless, the scale of the tower remains intact and a number of wall plaques survive from the medieval period. These commemorate the Lynch (Fig. 16) and FitzGerald families and include the coat of arms of King Henry VIII and a Latin scroll that reads 'Long live the King of England, France and Lord of Ireland' (Fig. 17). During the nineteenth century a wooden shopfront was inserted at ground-floor level, and around 1933 the ground-floor windows and door were replaced by an arcade of round-headed doors and windows. The tower-house is now in use as a bank. Inside the entrance hall is a carved stone fireplace, removed from an adjoining house, with an inscribed date of 1629.

Fig. 14—The Lynch tower-house, with altered windows and imposed Georgian character.

Above: Fig. 15—Blocked-up medieval window on the Shop Street elevation of the Lynch tower-house.

Below left: Fig. 16—Circular stone plaque bearing the coat of arms of the Lynch family on the wall of the Lynch tower-house.

Below right: Fig. 17—Coat of arms of Henry VIII and a Latin scroll that reads 'Long live the King of England' on the Lynch tower-house.

6. Medieval house, Quay Street, *c.* 1500

The restored medieval house on the corner of Quay Street and Quay Lane is one of a number of domestic buildings constructed in Galway during the medieval period. Erected around the beginning of the sixteenth century, it had become derelict over the years and was purchased by the Aran Sweater Market in 2016. The new owners initiated a detailed archaeological investigation of the site, followed by the splendid restoration of the building, which was completed in 2018 (Fig. 18). During the investigation, the remains of a partially preserved twelfth-century structure were discovered at basement level. This was part of a castle built by the Norman warlord Richard de Burgo in 1124 and was demolished around 1280. As part of the restoration programme, the twelfth-century ruins were conserved and visitors can view them through a glass screen (Fig. 19). Today the two-storey Quay Street elevation has a sequence of windows on both floor levels, each divided into double panes with re-crafted

Left: Fig. 18—The restored medieval house at the junction of Quay Street and Quay Lane.

Opposite, top: Fig. 19—Remnants of a recently discovered twelfth-century building, displayed under a glass viewing panel in the floor of the restored medieval house on Quay Street and Quay Lane.

Opposite lower left: Fig. 20—Restored arched doorway and mouldings of the medieval house, Quay Street.

Opposite lower right: Fig. 21—Restored gable elevation of the medieval house, Quay Lane.

cut-stone framing and mullions. The curved central doorway with its cut-stone surrounds and overhead hood-moulding was also restored (Fig. 20), as were the cut-stone quoins at the corner of the block between Quay Street and Quay Lane. The Quay Lane elevation is similar to that on Quay Street, except for the high-pitched gable with its extra level of windows. Here the re-crafted windows and central doorway are similar in design to those on Quay Street, with the addition of the attic windows on the gable (Fig. 21). The restored building is now used for retail purposes.

7. Medieval house, Kirwan's Lane, 1575

The former medieval house on Kirwan's Lane is another example of a domestic building and dates from around 1575 (Fig. 22). It is one of a number of adjacent medieval buildings on the street, offering a unique example of how a section of the Galway streetscape appeared during the sixteenth and seventeenth centuries. It is the most intact example in the lane, but the interior was remodelled as a pub in the 1990s and has been much altered. The three-storey building, which once acted as a convent, has an arched door and double-pane windows at ground level (Fig. 23). There was once a second, smaller entrance arch, but that was converted into a window sometime in the past. Overhead there are three large similar windows on each level, divided into six panes by cut-stone mullions, transoms and surrounds (Fig. 24). The rooftop dormer windows are a later addition. The adjoining house has been considerably altered, but a section of the original elevation that survives has a cut-stone framed doorway with a smaller but blocked-up archway immediately beside it (Fig. 25). Overhead, the surviving section of the first floor has a pair of windows with cut-stone mullions, transoms and surrounds. A third house in the street has again been much altered. The stone walling partly survives, as do the double arched entrance doorways, but the upper-floor windows have been replaced by wooden sashes set into the cut-stone surrounds.

Fig. 22—Adjoining examples of Galway's sixteenth-century houses, Kirwan's Lane.

Above left: Fig. 23—Arched doorway of medieval house, Kirwan's Lane.

Above right: Fig. 24—Cut-stone upper-floor windows with mullions and transoms, Kirwan's Lane.

Below: Fig. 25—Cut-stone arched doorways and first-floor cut-stone mullioned and transomed windows on Kirwan's Lane.

8. Corner house, Spanish Parade, *c.* 1600

The stone corner house with its slated gable roof to the front on Spanish Parade dates from around 1600 and is an excellent example of one of the many sixteenth-century houses that made up the medieval streetscapes of Galway (Fig. 26). The elevation consists of carefully cut and uniformly laid stone blocks. At ground level the skilfully constructed cut-stone pointed-arched entrance at the front has moulded sides with decorated and chamfered bases (Fig. 27). Overhead, most of the original windows on the upper floors have been replaced by later sash windows, except for the double ogee-headed window on the side elevation (Fig. 28) and a small attic window on the front gable. The building is now in use as a restaurant.

Fig. 26—The gable-fronted corner house on Spanish Parade dates from around 1600 and is typical of many of the houses of this period that once existed in Galway

Fig. 27—Cut-stone entrance door of the corner house on Spanish Parade, with moulded sides and chamfered bases.

Fig. 28—Mullioned and transomed window, corner house, Spanish Parade.

9. Medieval house front, Eyre Square, 1627

The reassembled doorway and first-floor window of a seventeenth-century house stand in Eyre Square as a memorial to the rich domestic architecture of Galway. The doorway was moved from the original site of the Brown family home, which had been demolished, and was re-erected against the rendered panel in the Square in 1905 (Fig. 29). The splendid example of a decorated doorway has a flat-headed semicircular arch flanked by moulded columns, with an overhead panel inscribed in Latin with Psalm 127:1: 'If the Lord does not build a house, than those who build it work in vain'. Above this, the window base carries a pair of stone plaques. These include the coats of arms of the house-owners, Martin Brown and Marie Lynch, and celebrate their marriage in 1627 (Fig. 30). Overhead, a splayed and projecting oriel window is divided into vertical panes by cut-stone mullions and a single transom. The house front was initially erected to act as the entrance gate to Eyre Square, although the railings that enclosed the rest of the square were subsequently removed.

Opposite above: Fig. 29—Doorway and upper level of the Brown family house of 1625, re-erected as the gateway to Eyre Square in 1905.

Opposite below: Fig. 30—Coats of arms of the Brown and Lynch families on the re-erected doorway and window, Eyre Square.

10. Lynch Memorial Wall, Lombard Street, 1624

The Lynch Memorial Wall on Lombard Street was erected in 1855 in the form of a stone house gable featuring two windows, two doorways and a keystone that had been collected from elsewhere and reassembled to suggest the elevation of a medieval house (Fig. 31). Over one of the blocked-up doorways is a carved skull-and-crossbones plaque, said to have once stood over the doorway of another house (Fig. 32). According to a seventeenth-century tradition, the Memorial Wall marks the spot where Walter Lynch Fitz Stephen was hanged for the murder of a stranger by the chief magistrate and mayor of the city: his own father, James Lynch Fitz Stephen.

Fig. 31—Lynch Memorial Wall, assembled from medieval house fragments in 1855, on Lombard Street.

Fig. 32—Skull-and-crossbones plaque on the Lynch Memorial Wall on Lombard Street, said to mark the spot where Walter Lynch Fitz Stephen was executed by his father for murder.

11. Former corner house, Abbeygate Street and Lower William Street, 1500 and 1850

In a common practice, a large number of medieval Galway houses were extensively refurbished during the nineteenth century, when the medieval character of the street front was replaced by Georgian features of the eighteenth and nineteenth centuries. In these cases the stone elevations were coated with plain rendering, effectively hiding much of the original medieval character. Furthermore, the original medieval windows were replaced by Georgian-style examples. The three-storey corner house at the intersection of Abbeygate Street and Lower William Street, for example, dates from around 1500, but it was modified around 1850 when the render was applied to the street fronts, the windows were replaced by up-and-down sliding sashes, and large ground-level shop windows were inserted across the fronts and around the curved apex of the wedge-shaped building (Fig. 33), which was converted to retail use. The one element of the medieval elevation to survive is the top-floor window on the Lower William Street elevation. This is now set into a plain projecting panel and features a medieval double-ogee pane in a rectangular opening with moulded edging, a flat decorated head and a hood-moulding (Fig. 34).

Opposite: Fig. 33—The Georgian street elevation of the corner house at the junction of Abbeygate Street and William Street dates from around 1850 and disguises the sixteenth-century origins of the building.

Above: Fig. 34—Medieval double-ogee window, Abbeygate Street and William Street corner house.

12. The Martin house, Cross Street and Quay Street, 1575 and 1860

The Martin house on the corner of Cross Street and Quay Street is another example of the replacement of the original medieval character. The house was once the home of Richard Martin, commonly known as 'Humanity Dick' for his work in the prevention of animal cruelty. The three-storey house with its gable end on Cross Street dates from around 1575 and was remodelled around 1880, when it was given a Georgian-style front. This included the insertion of the ground-level display windows, the plain rendering of the upper levels and the replacement of the windows on all floors, including the gable (Fig. 35). Two significant original medieval elements were, however, left in place: the upper-floor corner oriel window and the round-headed archway on Cross Street. The oriel window sits on a projecting three-sided base with cut-stone framing and six-pane mullion and the transom of the Cross Street elevation has a moulded semicircular arch, moulded uprights, and square head.

Opposite: Fig. 35—The Martin corner house at the junction of Cross Street and Quay Street dates from around 1575 and was given a Georgian-style elevation in 1860.

Above: Fig. 36—The cut-stone corner oriel window on the upper level of the Martin house, on the corner of Cross Street and Quay Street, survives from the medieval period.

Georgian Galway

During the eighteenth and nineteenth centuries the medieval streetscape of Galway was altered, and over time the medieval buildings were replaced by or remodelled as Georgian-style buildings. These new Georgian buildings were laid out in narrow plots that opened directly onto the streets—a spatial arrangement that still forms the main framework and character of Galway's historic core. This Georgian style of architecture originated in Renaissance Italy and spread all across Europe, reaching Galway during the eighteenth century. The characteristic features of these Georgian buildings included stone or rendered street fronts with an emphasis on vertical proportions, arched doorways and temple-fronted public buildings. The vertically proportioned windows are a particular feature of the Georgian period. These consist of tall, slim openings with sliding sashes, often divided into multiple small panes—usually six in each sash. Another characteristic feature of many Georgian town houses is the change in floor heights. The ground- and first-floor levels are similar, but the second- and third-floor ceiling heights are often reduced incrementally. This change in height is reflected in the different window heights: the ground- and first-floor window heights are similar, while the upper-floor windows decrease in height.

13. Mayoral house, St Augustine Street, 1760

The mayoral house on St Augustine Street dates from 1760 and is one of the earliest examples of a Georgian building to appear in Galway city. It was built as the official home of the mayor and was positioned on St Augustine Street so as to offer a closing vista to the perpendicularly aligned Cross Street (Fig. 37). The Palladian-style block is four storeys high over a basement. The street elevation is marked by finely cut ashlar masonry and is divided into three bays, defined by quoins. The wide central bay features the entrance, with a standard Georgian window on either side. The cut-stone door-case has moulded surrounds with a flat head and a curved moulded pediment overhead (Fig. 38). The panelled double door has a rectangular decorated fanlight. The stone entrance steps have low side walls capped with decorated railings that extend across the front of the building to protect the low-level basement area. The standard Georgian windows are vertically proportioned, with replacement large-paned sashes. These are arranged so that the windows on each floor level are positioned one above the other, each with moulded surrounds. Today the mayoral house is in office use and, with the exception of the replacement windows, offers an intact and impressive example of Galway's Georgian architecture.

Above left: Fig. 37—Three-bay symmetrical elevation of the former mayoral house on St Augustine Street, one of the finest Georgian houses in Galway.

Right: Fig. 38—The cut-stone moulded door-case, curved pediment, stone steps and metal handrails present an impressive and formal entrance to the mayoral house, St Augustine Street.

14. Former house, Williamsgate Street, 1750

The extremely wide-fronted three-storey stone house on Williamsgate Street dates from 1750 and has in the past been divided into independent sections, particularly at ground level, where the original elevation has been converted to retail use. Here the original window openings have been considerably widened and a range of shop fronts inserted. These include a pair of display windows, a central shop door set into a plain stone surround and an overhead fascia, with a plain doorway to the upper levels on one side. On the two upper levels the original sashes of the nine Georgian windows have been removed and replaced with large-paned sashes (Fig. 39). The most significant feature of the elevation is, however, the oculus, or circular window, at the midpoint of both the first and the second floor (Fig. 40). Here the original sashes have been replaced, although their cut-stone surrounds and wedge-shaped quadrants survive as significant Georgian features.

Fig. 39—Replacement Georgian windows of the former Williamsgate Street house with cut-stone surrounds.

Fig. 40—The cut-stone surrounds and wedge-shaped quadrants of the circular replacement windows mark the midpoint of the former Williamsgate Street house.

15. The Joyce house, Church Lane, 1786

The three-storey stone house owned by the Joyce family stands on the narrow Church Lane and was probably built around 1786 on the site of an earlier medieval building (Fig. 41). The rough cut-stone wall has Georgian windows on all three levels, with flat arches and sliding six-paned sashes. At some period the original door-case was removed and replaced by a central double door and two narrower side doors, all framed in plain render. A low carriage arch that cuts through the wall on the left side of the block originally provided access to the rear of the building. An interesting feature of the elevation is the elaborately carved plaque with the Joyce family coat of arms and 1786 date (Fig. 42). This is positioned over the doorway but in a curiously off-centre position. The building is now in office use.

Fig. 41 —The Joyce house on Church Lane has stone walling, Georgian windows and a slated roof.

Fig. 42—The Joyce family coat of arms and history plaque is curiously placed off-centre, just above the line of the entrance door on Church Lane.

16. Former warehouse, Kirwan's Lane, 1790

In addition to housing, a number of Georgian industrial buildings were also completed within Galway's historic core, including the former warehouse on Kirwan's Lane. This impressive stone-built warehouse extends over six storeys in height at the midpoint turn on Kirwan's Lane. Here it acts as an end vista from Cross Street and reflects the significant level of commercial enterprise in the eighteenth-century city (Fig. 43). The structure was built in 1790 and, although it once acted as a chemical store, the block was recently converted to office and restaurant use and a roof-level dormer storey added. The many warehouse windows of the building are square, with cut-stone flat-arched heads. The original windows now carry replacement sashes. The grid-like arrangement of these small windows adds a dramatic chequer pattern to both the warehouse elevation and the overall streetscape. The ground level had an arrangement of doorways and windows in addition to a wide coach arch to one side (Fig. 44). The coach arch has been retained and the doors and windows replaced with glazed panels and doors. The gable end of the warehouse originally had a doorway on each of the floor levels that allowed goods to be hoisted into position and into the warehouse from ground level. These doorways have recently been converted into balconies by the installation of glazed doorways to the various levels and the addition of semicircular metal platforms and railings (Fig. 45).

Fig. 43—The former warehouse on Kirwan's Lane has a stone elevation, with the industrial-sized windows arranged in a chequer fashion.

Fig. 44—The carefully cut stone coach arch at the side of the Kirwan's Lane former warehouse offers an example of the high standard of eighteenth-century stone craftsmanship.

Fig. 45—The gable elevation of the Kirwan's Lane former warehouse features rounded balconies and glazed doorways on the three upper levels.

17. Former warehouse, St Augustine Street, 1795

The former warehouse on St Augustine Street was built in 1795 and is more elaborate in the form and quality of its stonework than the Kirwan's Lane example. The wide block is four storeys high over a basement, with a cut-stone parapet and an attic storey which was added in 1990 (Fig. 46) when the block was redeveloped to accommodate apartments, a clinic and a club. A striking feature of the block is the former central loading bay. This has been reformed as a tall glazed screen with a gable at the new attic level (Fig. 47). Underneath, the ground-level carriage arch and two smaller flanking entrance arches are linked by string-courses at the base of the cut-stone arches. All three archways have been given panelled replacement doors with semicircular fanlights. The stepped accesses to the doorways are framed within metal railings that extend across the front of the block to shield the lower basement-level area. On the upper floors the vertically proportioned window openings decrease in height on each floor level and now have Georgian-style replacement sashes.

Fig. 46—The stone-fronted former warehouse on St Augustine Street has a central triple-arch entrance and a glazed screen, in addition to a range of Georgian-proportioned replacement windows.

Fig. 47—The centre point of the former St Augustine Street warehouse is emphasised by the tall glazed inserted screen and the three linked arched doorways of the ground level.

18. Joyce town house, St Augustine Street, 1795

The Joyce house is one of a terrace of town houses on St Augustine Street and dates from 1795. The term 'town house' relates to the tall and narrow form of such houses, which often had a standard internal layout. This took the form of a room to the front and a room to the rear, with the entrance hall and staircase to one side. The terraced ashlar house was built by John Joyce, a Galway merchant; it stands four storeys high over a basement and has all the characteristic features of the eighteenth-century Georgian town house (Fig. 48). The semi-circular door, set into a recessed archway with plain rendered jambs and a double arch (Fig. 49), is reached by steps and a landing that spans the basement area. The sides of the platform have decorated railings that extend across the front of the house, separating the footpath from the lower-level basement area below. The window arrangements follow the standard Georgian practice, including a reduction in height on each floor and vertically proportioned sliding sashes divided into small panes. The window pattern has three windows spread across the front of the upper floors and two at the ground and basement levels, with the windows positioned directly above the ones below. Today the Joyce town house is in office use.

Fig. 48—The Joyce town house on St Augustine Street has a sequence of Georgian windows with the door-case to one side.

Fig. 49—The arched entrance door and semicircular fanlight of the Joyce town house on St Augustinian Street, set into the recessed and rendered door-case.

19. Rendered town house, Eyre Square, 1800

The terraced town house on Eyre Square, standing to three storeys over a basement, was built around 1800. The rendered elevation, facing the square, has been lined and scribed to imitate stonework. This is one of a cluster of colour-washed houses on the square that make up a particularly elegant streetscape, offering a lighter visual image than the more common stone-faced elevations of the typical Galway house (Fig. 50). The windows of the house follow the usual Georgian pattern of horizontal and vertical spacing, each window with large double-pane sashes. The semicircular arched doorway to one side has a semicircular fanlight, with cut-stone steps leading from the footpath level (Fig. 51) and cast-iron side railings that separate the basement area from the footpath and extend across the front of the house. Today the slate-roofed town house is in commercial use.

Fig. 50—The town house on Eyre Square has a three-storey rendered elevation, lined and inscribed to imitate cut stone, and a standard arrangement of Georgian double-pane sliding sashes spaced at equal intervals across the elevation.

Fig. 51—The replacement entrance doorway of the rendered town house on Eyre Square is set into a splayed archway.

20. End-of-terrace town house, Eyre Square, 1800

The corner terraced house on Eyre Square, three storeys high over a basement, dates from around 1800 and is similar in many respects to the nearby rendered town house (No. 19). It has three Georgian windows of equal height that stretch across the front of the upper storeys, a round-headed door-case to one side, and stone entrance steps and cast-iron railings to the basement area at the front; like No. 19, its rendered elevation is scribed in imitation stonework (Fig. 52). A number of embellishments have also been incorporated into the elevation, including moulded window and door surrounds (Fig. 53) and solid rendered quoins at either side of the building.

Fig. 52—The terraced town house on Eyre Square is rendered, with moulded window surrounds, arched doorway to one side and solid quoins at either end.

Fig. 53—The terraced town house on Eyre Square has single-pane sliding sashes, framed by moulded surrounds.

21. Bank of Ireland building, Eyre Square, 1810

The Bank of Ireland building on Eyre Square was designed for the bank by the architect James Cusack and built in 1810. The wide, two-storey building, which faces the square, has a cut-stone ground floor and a lined and scribed rendered upper floor, with slightly recessed bays at either end (Fig. 54). The cut-stone lower level has an arcade of seven semicircular arches across the front. The end bays have a panel door set into an inner arch, and between the bays are a series of round-headed Georgian windows, also set into inner arches. The rendered upper level has rectangular windows, placed one above each of the ground-level arches. These have double sashes with moulded surrounds. Overhead, the slate roof is screened by a moulded parapet with a centrally placed clock face and bank sign (Fig. 55). At ground level a decorated cast-iron railing with a low-level stone plinth stretches across the front of the building (Fig. 56). Internally, the nineteenth-century arrangement remains intact, particularly the ground-level banking hall. Directly opposite the bank is the restored medieval house front memorial (No. 9 above) and the Galway Hooker sculpture, both in the paved area of Eyre Square. The vibrant copper boat memorial was erected in 1984 and represents a traditional Galway hooker in full sail (Fig. 57).

Fig. 54—The arcaded stone and rendered two-storey elevation of the Bank of Ireland building faces onto the north side of Eyre Square.

Fig. 55—The rooftop clock of the Bank of Ireland building on Eyre Square is raised on a cut-stone central panel inscribed with the name of the bank.

Fig. 56—An ornate cast-iron railing leads to the doorway of the Bank of Ireland building on Eyre Square and extends across the front on a cut-stone plinth.

Fig. 57—The memorial on Eyre Square represents the sails of the traditional Galway hooker—a dramatic interpretation of wind, sea and form.

22. Former courthouse, Courthouse Square, 1810

The former city and county courthouse is one of Galway's finest Georgian public buildings. It was built in 1810 on the site of a medieval Franciscan friary to the design of the architect Sir Richard Morrison. The rear cut-stone elevation was formally aligned on the central axis of the Salmon Weir Bridge over the River Corrib (Fig. 58). The triple-gabled river front has a recessed central bay, with rows of standard Georgian windows on each of the three levels and a clock face in the gable. The slightly lower side bays have a round-headed door at ground level and a round-headed window on the upper floors. The more elaborate main elevation of the block faces the small, landscaped Courthouse Square and features a single-storey open portico, laid out in the form of a Greek or Roman temple front (Fig. 59). This has four tall columns with a decorated entablature and moulded cornice, and is one of the earliest Galway examples of the use of the temple front design. Behind the portico is a central doorway and four round-headed archways at ground level. The archways on either side of the doorway have round-headed windows, while the outer archways are blind with rectangular decorated panels immediately above. There is a circular cast-iron postbox in one corner of the courtyard, inscribed with the George V emblem surmounted by a crown and a 1916 date (Fig. 60). In contrast to the formality of the main elevations, the two cut-stone side elevations have an irregular arrangement of blind arches and Georgian windows.

Fig. 58—The gabled riverside elevation of the former courthouse on Courthouse Square is aligned on the central axis of the Salmon Weir Bridge.

Above: Fig. 59—The entrance elevation of the former courthouse on Courthouse Square opens onto the landscaped courtyard and has an open projecting portico with tall columns and side wings, the latter with blank arches.

Right: Fig. 60—The 1916 circular postbox with the crown and 'GR' initials stands in one corner of the landscaped courtyard of the former courthouse.

23. Former town hall, Courthouse Square, 1820

The former town hall on Courthouse Square has a chequered history. It was built in 1820 and went on to serve as a courthouse, a town hall, a cinema and a theatre. The architect Alexander Hay laid out the cut-stone and rendered building in the form of a single-storey front section and a much larger double-storey back section, facing the small landscaped courtyard between the building and the former courthouse (No. 22 above). The symmetrically arranged front is by far the most elaborate, with a recessed portico flanked on either side by a side bay and a moulded parapet (Fig. 61). The distinctive open temple-fronted portico has four columns, an overhead moulded entablature (Fig. 62) and side bays with rusticated (open-jointed) masonry and wide windows. These windows have cambered arches and large, wedge-shaped arch stones; each has three vertical mullions and a deep transom, with large glazed panels in the lower section and small square panes above (Fig. 63). The side elevations of the front section are similarly elaborate, with rusticated masonry and camber-headed windows matching those on the front. The rendered elevations of the taller back block are, however, more modest and feature an irregular arrangement of vertically proportioned windows, blind arches, string-courses, quoins and moulded parapets.

Fig. 61—The single-storey front section of the former town hall faces onto the landscaped courtyard and features a temple-fronted portico and side bays.

Fig. 62—The open, recessed, temple-fronted portico of the former town hall has four round columns, a decorated entablature and a glazed entrance screen behind.

Fig. 63—The corner side bay of the entrance elevation of the former town hall has a large, intricate window design, with wedge-shaped arch stones, set into the rusticated masonry.

24. Shop, Williamsgate Street, 1820

This two-storey shop, built in 1820, is part of a wide commercial block fronting onto Williamsgate Street (Fig. 64). The box-framed ground-level shop front dates from the nineteenth century and features a central glazed entrance doorway, splayed display windows with wooden uprights and vertical ribbed side columns at either end. Above this the moulded fascia has a moulded cornice, carries the shop name and stretches across the full width of the building (Fig. 65). The stone upper level of the building has three standard Georgian windows spaced evenly across the front. Each of these has a moulded surround and sliding sashes, each with six panes and a slated roof overhead.

Fig. 64—The Williamsgate Street shop building has an attractive framed wooden shop front and display windows, with Georgian windows lined across the stone-faced upper level.

Fig. 65—The ribbed side column, head and moulded fascia of the Williamsgate Street shop.

25. Former warehouse, Merchant's Road, 1820

The date-stone over the entrance to the former Niland House warehouse indicates a date of 1820 for this building on Merchant's Road near Galway Harbour (Fig. 66). This is one of a number of warehouses around the Merchant's Road area built to cater to the harbour trade during the nineteenth century, although their importance diminished with the coming of the railway to the city in 1851. The scale and bulk of the warehouse building form a significant presence on the Merchant's Road streetscape and demonstrate the powerful nineteenth-century mercantile legacy of the city. The coursed random rubble stone building is five storeys high, and an attic story was recently added. The block has a range of almost-square window openings on all levels, now glazed with replacement windows. Today the recently installed rounded balconies face the street and represent a prominent feature of the Niland House block's recent conversion to residential apartments (Fig. 67). These were inserted into the vertical openings that once provided access to the different floor levels of the building. Glazed doors were fitted into the openings, and projecting balconies and metal railings were added. The two eliptical arched entrance doors to the block have block and start cut-stone surrounds and wedge-shaped keystones inscribed with the coat of arms and the initials of the builder, as well as the construction date (Fig. 68).

Fig. 66—The cut-stone wedge-shaped keystone over the entrance to Niland House on Merchant's Road bears the coat of arms of the builder and the 1820 construction date.

Fig. 67—The tall stone former warehouse on Merchant's Road has been successfully converted to residential apartments.

Fig. 68—The cut-stone doorway of the former warehouse has an eliptical arch, raised block and start cut-stone surrounds, wedged-shaped arch stones, a central keystone, and a glazed and sheeted replacement door.

26. Semi-detached town house, Eyre Square, 1824

The corner house on Eyre Square is one of a pair dating from 1824 and is one of the most significant Georgian town houses in Galway. It stands four storeys high over the basement and is two window bays wide, with a pitched slated roof (Fig. 69). The standard window openings are Georgian in scale, although the sliding sashes are replacements. The highly crafted cut-stone door-case projects slightly forward and has a triangular open-based pediment, with elaborate decorative stonework carried on a pair of rounded columns (Fig. 70). The double-leaf panelled door has a semicircular fanlight, and the house front has decorated metal railings that lead to the door and continue across the front to shield the footpath from the basement level below.

Fig. 69—Elevation of the semi-detached town house on Eyre Square, with the Georgian window openings, replacement sashes, date-stone, and the cut-stone door-case to one side.

Fig. 70—Finely carved cut-stone door-case of the semi-detached town house on Eyre Square, with half-round side columns and a triangular open-based pediment.

27. Augustinian priory, St Augustine Street, 1830

The Augustinian priory was built in 1830 to provide administrative and residential accommodation for the community of the adjoining Augustinian church on St Augustine Street. The building was probably designed by the architect Michael Brophy Moran, who seems to have worked exclusively for Augustinian communities across Ireland. The symmetrically arranged stone building is three storeys high over a basement, with the tops of the basement windows projecting slightly above the footpath level (Fig. 71). The original centrally placed entrance door-case has recently been replaced with a panelled door, narrow side lights and overhead decorated radial fanlight, all set into the curved archway. In an unusual example, the doorway is reached by a sideways arrangement of cut-stone steps with cast-iron railings to one side. On the three upper levels of the building the uniformly spaced replacement windows are set into the Georgian-proportioned window openings with moulded surrounds.

Fig. 71 — The Augustinian priory building, adjacent to the Augustinian church on St Augustine Street, with the doorway set into a shallow curved recess, a flight of stone side steps and cast-iron railings leading to the doorway.

28. The United Methodist and Presbyterian church, Queen Street, 1835

In 1750 a small Methodist Society was formed in Galway, and around 1835 a Georgian-style chapel was opened on the corner of Queen Street and Victoria Place. In 1989 the Methodist and Presbyterian communities united and began worshipping together in the Queen Street church. The symmetrical stone street elevation of the church faces down Victoria Place, where it acts as an end vista to the street. The two-storey block has a triangular gabled roof and three round-headed windows with replacement Georgian sashes, two at ground level and one on the first floor, all with wedge-shaped arch stones (Fig. 72). The lower-level windows have overhead rectangular plaques, and the arch of the upper window breaks the base line of the triangular gable. The gabled single-storey front porch dates from later in the nineteenth century and, in contrast to the Georgian style of the main block, was built in an imitation Gothic style, with a pointed-arched door and low-level corner buttresses (Fig. 73). Internally, the church has plastered and painted walls with round-headed windows. The adjoining three-storey schoolhouse seems to have been squeezed in between the side of the church and the adjoining building on Victoria Place. The schoolhouse also has a gabled front but an unusual entrance arrangement: a flight of stairs that starts on one side of the church front and extends upwards to the round-headed school door on the first-floor level (Fig. 74). The ground- and first-floor Georgian windows of the school also have round heads, while those on the upper floor have flat heads. Like the church, the windows of the schoolhouse are replacements. At roof level, the corner of the triangular gable butts against that of the church.

Fig. 72—The distinctive Georgian gable front of the United Methodist and Presbyterian church on Queen Street faces down Victoria Place.

Right: Fig. 73—The projecting entrance porch of the United Methodist and Presbyterian church was built in an imitation Gothic style, with a pointed arch, buttresses and a panelled door.

Below: Fig. 74—The narrow-fronted school building sits between the United Methodist and Presbyterian church on Queen Street and the adjoining building on Victoria Place and is accessed at first-floor level by a stairway.

29. Terraced town house, Spanish Parade, 1837

This stone house is one of five matching terraced town houses, built around 1837, positioned on the dog-leg angle of Spanish Parade (Fig. 75). It is three storeys high over a basement, with a recently restored pitched slated roof. The Georgian window pattern is two bays wide, with cut-stone surrounds and flat lintels, although the Georgian sliding sashes are replacements. The entrance door and narrow side lights, also replacements, are set in a segmental arch with block and start cut-stone surrounds and a wedge-shaped keystone (Fig. 76). The house has decorated railings leading to the doorway and stretching across the house front.

Fig. 75—The stone terraced town house on Spanish Parade features cut-stone window openings, arched door surrounds and replacement joinery.

Fig. 76—The replacement door, frame and fanlight of the terraced town house on Spanish Parade are set into a cut-stone segmental arch with block and start surrounds.

30. Galway railway station, Station Road, 1840

The Galway railway station, now called Ceannt Station, was designed as the terminal of the Midland Great Western Railway by the noted railway architect John Skipton Mulvany, and was constructed on lands south of Eyre Square that had been reclaimed from the sea during the nineteenth century. The Georgian-inspired complex was extensive and included the passenger arrival and departure block, the train shed, an engine shed and the hotel at one end, facing onto Eyre Square (No. 33 below). The single-storey-over-basement passenger block faces onto Station Road and has an extended symmetrical elevation incorporating a pattern of receding and projecting bays, built with ashlar masonry (Fig. 77). The block has replacement Georgian windows on both levels, with a high-level corbelled cornice and a plain roof pediment, as well as an elaborate cast-iron railing at ground level (Fig. 78). In the centre, cut-stone steps lead up to the recessed double-door passenger entrance bay, which has an overhead stone canopy supported on four curved cast-iron brackets. The entrance bay is flanked on both sides by forward-projecting side bays, each with a pair of replacement Georgian windows set into square-headed recessed openings (Fig. 79). Internally, the entrance block houses a ticket office and administrative offices, as well as retail and commercial units and access to the train platform, where the steel-framed roof and metal decking are recent additions.

Fig. 77—The cut-stone elevation of the Galway railway station block has a sequence of alternating bays, Georgian windows and cast-iron railings that extend along Station Road.

Fig. 78—The recessed entrance bay and double doorway to the Galway railway station provide access to the train platforms and mark the centre point of the Station Road elevation.

Fig. 79—The window openings of the Galway railway station on Station Road feature replacement sashes set into the ashlar stonework.

31. Hibernian House, Eyre Square, 1840

The tall and imposing former County Club clubhouse, now known as Hibernian House, was built on the north side of Eyre Square in 1840. During the twentieth century the interior of the clubhouse was totally refurbished, and an extensive office development was built immediately behind and attached to the original clubhouse block. The original Eyre Square elevation was recently refurbished and the block is now in commercial use. The extravagantly arranged Eyre Square cut-stone elevation is divided into a series of panels by full-height columns and an arrangement of replacement Georgian windows on all levels, including square and round-headed sashes as well as square attic windows, above which a slated mansard story with small round-headed windows has recently been added (Fig. 80). In addition, a continuous cornice stretches across the full width of the block, dividing the first-floor level from the overhead attic-floor level. The centre point of the building is emphasised at ground level by the open temple-style entrance porch that faces the square. This has a double pair of rounded columns that support the entablature and flat moulded roof (Fig. 81). Sitting prominently on the square, opposite the entrance porch, is the carved stone figure of Liam Mellows, a War of Independence revolutionary figure, mounted on a cut-stone plinth, unveiled in 1957 (Fig. 82).

Fig. 80—The former County Club clubhouse faces onto Eyre Square with a range of characteristic Georgian elements, including cut-stone masonry, sash windows and an open temple-style entrance portico.

Fig. 81—The open, cut-stone temple-like portico faces Eyre Square and acts as the formal entrance to the former County Club clubhouse.

Fig. 82—The 1957 stone memorial to the executed revolutionary leader Liam Mellows stands on a tall plinth on Eyre Square facing the front elevation of the former County Club.

32. Franciscan church, St Francis Street, 1849

In 1660 the first Franciscan church on Francis Street was built on the site of the present church. This was rebuilt in 1849 and laid out in a richly finished Georgian style, designed by the architect James Cusack in the form of a Greco-Roman temple. Cusack positioned the church so that the temple-fronted portico, or formal entrance porch, projected beyond the splayed street line and was visible from along the street (Fig. 83). The two-storey cut-stone portico was given four round columns, an elaborate entablature and a moulded triangular pediment mounted by a cross-shaped finial. This smooth cut-stone finish contrasts with the rougher stonework of the remainder of the church elevations. Beneath the portico the church has an arrangement of three doorways: a flat-headed main door flanked on either side by round-headed side doors. Above these is a central round-headed window flanked on either side by a pair of round-headed blind arches. Internally, the church has a fine plastered interior with a central nave, two side aisles, an ornate plastered barrel-vaulted ceiling and a dome (Fig. 84). The tall nave is separated from the side aisles by an open arcade of circular columns with high-level semicircular windows. The coffered dome over the altar is carried on vaulted angles and has a sequence of decorated panels on the underside (Fig. 85). The tall background panel to the main altar has a broken arched pediment carried on a pair of rounded columns—a feature balanced at the far end of the nave by a high-level wooden-framed organ gallery.

Fig. 83—The projecting double-height cut-stone portico of St Francis's Abbey Church is a prominent feature of St Francis Street.

Fig. 84—The interior of St Francis's Abbey Church on St Francis Street has an attractive range of Georgian features, including the plastered nave, side aisles and barrel-vaulted ceiling.

Fig. 85—The panelled and ribbed decorated dome over the sanctuary area of the nave of St Francis's Abbey Church.

33. Hotel, Eyre Square, 1850

The large, elaborate hotel building on Eyre Square was designed by the architect John Shipton Mulvany and built in 1850 as part of the Galway railway station complex. Today the building remains a major architectural set piece that takes up most of the south side of Eyre Square (Fig. 86). It was originally called the Railway Hotel, later the Great Southern Hotel and recently the Meyrick—after James Meyrick, one of the individuals involved in the laying-out of Eyre Square. The hotel block is four storeys high over the basement, and a flat-roofed attic storey has recently been added. The complex elevation to the square is divided into five bays, with the central and end bays projecting slightly forwards. It features rusticated ground-level stonework, plain ashlar on the other floors and cut-stone moulded linear bands that highlight the various floor levels between the rows of Georgian windows with their replacement sashes (Fig. 87)—a vertical effect emphasised by the projecting cornice underneath the new attic storey. Entrance to the three side-by-side hotel doors is by means of cut-stone steps with cast-iron and brass handrails and ornate cast-iron lamps mounted on cut-stone pedestals (Fig. 88). Across the front an ornate cast-iron railing on a cut-stone plinth separates the footpath from the lower basement area. Internally, the basement holds the service areas, the ground floor the reception and public rooms, and the upper floors the guest accommodation, where much of the original interior plasterwork and fittings survive.

Fig. 86—The scale, form and craftsmanship of the hotel play a major part in the spatial quality of Eyre Square.

Fig. 87—The stone moulded linear bands on the street front of the hotel on Eyre Square highlight the various floor levels and the uniform window patterns.

Fig. 88—The triple entrance doors to the hotel on Eyre Square are set between rusticated panels with stone access steps, brass and cast-iron handrails, and cast-iron light fittings on stone pedestals.

34. Former market house, Eyre Square, 1863

The cut-stone former market house was designed by the architect William Caldbeck and laid out on one corner of Eyre Square in 1863, adjacent to the hotel. Although similar in complexity to the hotel design, it is more modest in scale. The building has had many former uses, including as the market house and as a bank, and is currently in office and commercial use. The symmetrical Georgian cut-stone elevation stands four storeys tall over the basement, with rusticated masonry at ground level and plain ashlar on the upper floors (Fig. 89). The Georgian windows on each of the floors have large panes. Those on the ground level are round-headed, the first-floor examples have projecting pediments and the top-floor windows have cambered heads. The panelled entrance doors at either end of the elevation have semicircular fanlights, rusticated columns and projecting canopies, on top of which sits an elaborate carved first-floor balcony serving a first-floor window (Fig. 90). There is a single-story curved wing on either end with former carriage arches, now glazed in (Fig. 91). The market house block also features string-courses, quoins, a bracketed frieze, a plain cut-stone parapet and low stone baluster front railings.

Fig. 89—The cut-stone elevation of the former market house, with its side wings, Georgian windows, first-floor balconies and double entrance doors facing onto Eyre Square.

Fig. 90—The former market house has cut-stone entrance door-cases with rounded columns that support entablatures and first-floor balconies.

Fig. 91—The original coach arches of the former market house have recently been filled in with windows.

35. Town house, Dock Road, 1860

The end-of-terrace town house on Dock Road dates from around 1860. It overlooks the docks and is one of the few surviving examples of Galway's narrow town houses (Fig. 92). The rendered street front has a pair of standard Georgian sash windows on each of the three floors. These are framed with moulded surrounds and the original sliding sashes remain in place. The rendered elevation is lined and scribed to imitate stonework, with rendered quoins at each end. The elliptical-headed door and fanlight to one side of the house has a moulded surround with a wedge-shaped keystone. Internally, the house is laid out in the typical town house arrangement, with a room to the front, a room to the rear and a side entrance.

Opposite right: Fig. 92—The rendered Georgian town house on the Dock Road has moulded window surrounds and is one of the few surviving examples of the smaller Galway Georgian terraced town houses.

36. Former department store, William Street/Eglinton Street, 1860

The former department store, also called the Eglinton Building, on the corner of William Street and Eglinton Street dates from 1860 and is one of the first purpose-built department stores to be completed in Galway (Fig. 93). The architect may have been Edward Henry Carson, but this is uncertain. Initially known as 'Moons of Galway', the store is given landmark significance by its extended elevation and corner position on the busy shopping street. The elongated three-storey rendered and lined building extends along William Street, curves around the corner and returns along Eglinton Street. The ground level has a sequence of wide, flat-headed display windows set between pairs of decorated columns; overhead is an elaborately moulded fascia that extends across the entire front, with panels of decorated metal railings along the top. Above the shop level, fifteen round-headed Georgian windows with moulded surrounds stretch across the full width of the first-floor level, with a similar number of camber-arched Georgian windows on the upper level, the latter with a continuous sill. The roof line of the building is emphasised by the elaborately moulded rendered parapet. The outstanding feature of the elevation is the curved entrance corner, particularly when viewed from the approaching Williamsgate Street (Fig. 94). The curved entrance doorway to the store is set between a pair of double columns that support the moulded fascia overhead. Above this, the Georgian upper-floor windows are also set between full-height flat columns that extend from the top of the shop front fascia to the underside of the parapet (Fig. 95). Internally, the floors are in retail use.

Fig. 93—The three-storey elevation of the department store that curves around the junction of William Street and Eglinton Street features ground-level display windows, upper-level Georgian windows, and a moulded and decorated parapet.

Above: Fig. 94—The curved corner entrance to the department store on William Street and Eglinton Street is a notable city landmark, particularly when viewed from the approaching Williamsgate Street.

Right: Fig. 95—The first-floor Georgian windows of the department store at the junction of William Street and Eglinton Street have moulded and rounded heads, sliding sashes and small panes, while the upper-floor windows have similar but camber-headed sashes.

37. Colonial Building, Williamsgate Street/Eglinton Street, 1866

The large and complex Colonial Building, built in 1866, was designed by the architect Edward Henry Carson, father of unionist politician Sir Edward Carson. The layout of the building is complex and initially held the Galway Royal Institution, a social club, as well as a pub, retail stores, offices and three houses at the Eglinton Street end of the block. Today the corner section of the block that faces onto Williamsgate Street is in use as a restaurant. The remainder of the ground floor, including the former houses, is a pub, while the upper floors are in commercial and office use. The extremely long rendered building is three storeys high and—similar to the department store on the opposite side of the street (No. 36 above)—is rounded at the corner of Williamsgate Street and Eglinton Street, which features the main entrance door. The ground level of the block is divided into an arcade of elaborate bays of different-sized arched openings that extend along the Eglinton Street elevation (Fig. 96). All the arcade bays feature rusticated side panels, moulded arch surrounds, keystones and semicircular windows, although a few of the original windows have been replaced by doorways. A replacement window has, for instance, been inserted into the original carriage arch on the Eglinton Street elevation. In contrast to the complex design of the ground-level arcade, the first- and second-floor levels are restrained. A moulded projecting cornice separates the ground level from the first-floor level, above which the plain rendered upper levels of the block feature uniform Georgian sliding windows with moulded surrounds, spaced uniformly along both street fronts, with the plain overhead parapet at roof level.

Fig. 96—The ground-level arcade of the Colonial Building on the corner of Williamsgate Street and Eglinton Street has a series of moulded semicircular arches between rendered rusticated panels, with round-headed replacement windows between the panels.

38. Two-storey terraced house, St Francis Street, 1890

The two-storey house on St Francis Street dates from around 1890 and makes a significant contribution to a mixed terrace of Georgian houses forming the streetscape. The simple symmetrical elevation is rendered, with a central door-case, Georgian windows and a high-pitched slated roof (Fig. 97). The panelled door has a rectangular fanlight, a moulded surround, plain flat side columns, and a flat mounded pediment carried on scrolled brackets (Fig. 98). The two ground-floor standard Georgian sliding windows flank the doorway, while the evenly spaced upper-floor Georgian windows are arranged across the elevation, although the middle window is curiously positioned slightly off-centre of the hall door. The house is now in office use.

Fig. 97—The symmetrical two-storey house on St Francis Street is an important element in the mixed Georgian streetscape.

Fig. 98—The panelled door of the house on St Francis Street fits into a moulded surround, with plain side columns and a flat, mounded overhead pediment carried on scrolled brackets.

Victorian Galway

During the early part of the nineteenth century there was a change in architectural design, as the prevailing Georgian style was occasionally replaced by other forms based on the historical past, such as the Gothic Revival, following a fashion for all things medieval. Collectively such buildings can be classified as Victorian. The Georgian style was not, however, dispensed with, and the two styles often appeared in Galway—as elsewhere in Ireland—side by side.

39. Former Catholic cathedral, Middle Street, 1815

One of the earliest Victorian buildings to appear in Galway city was the former Catholic cathedral on the corner of Middle Street and Abbeygate Street (Fig. 99). This was designed in the Gothic Revival style by the architect James Cusack and built in 1815, in imitation of a medieval Gothic church building. With the completion of the new Galway Catholic cathedral in 1965 (No. 45 below), however, the former cathedral was no longer required, and the building was converted to retail and commercial use. Its double-height cut-stone Middle Street elevation features a central gabled bay, flanked on either side by narrow battlemented side bays, corner buttresses with decorated pinnacles, stepped parapet stones and a ball finial at the apex (Fig. 100). The five pointed-arched doorways are set into moulded rectangular panels, while the five pointed upper-floor windows are aligned on the doorways. The tall central window alone has cut-stone moulded surrounds. The original timber doors and windows on both levels were recently removed and the openings reglazed with replacement windows. An unusual feature of the elevation is the five stone-carved animals positioned above the window-heads. On the side elevation on Abbeygate Street the original pointed-arched timber doorway and windows have all been removed and, as on the Middle Street elevation, have been reglazed with replacement joinery (Fig. 101).

Above left: Fig. 99—The cut-stone entrance front of the former Galway cathedral on Market Street features pointed and moulded door and window openings, and replacement doors and windows.

Top right: Fig. 100—The gable of the former Galway cathedral on Market Street features corner buttresses, battlemented pediments, decorated pinnacles, a stepped parapet and a ball finial at the apex.

Bottom right: Fig. 101—The cut-stone Abbeygate Street side elevation of the former cathedral has a system of pointed arches on both floor levels, with replacement doors and windows.

40. Augustinian church, Middle Street, 1855

The Augustinian church on Middle Street is another of Galway's Gothic Revival buildings. This dates from 1855 and was built near the site of an earlier Franciscan church. It was designed by the architect Michael Brophy Moran, who seems to have worked exclusively for Augustinian communities all across Ireland. Work on the church started in 1855 and was completed four years later. Moran slotted the detached rectangular church into a tight site between Middle Street, Buttermilk Walk and St Augustine Street. The entrance front on Middle Street was laid out on a raised platform accessed by stone steps from the footpath and had a tall, gabled central bay with lower lean-to bays on either side, reflecting the roof line of the tall nave and lower side aisles of the building (Fig. 102). The central bay has a pointed entrance, a sheeted and strap-hinged door, and a small quatrefoil window high up on the triangular gable. The division between the central bay and the two side bays is marked by a square stepped buttress that extends up as far as the roof line. The side bays have similar doorways, each with an overhead circular leaded window (Fig. 103). At the rear of the church, the St Augustine Street elevation is similar to the front, with a triple-bay arrangement, square buttresses, a tall central leaded window and a pair of slim lancet windows. Linking the two streets, the plain Buttermilk Walk side aisle elevation has a sequence of pointed windows. The church interior has a tall central nave with lower side aisles on either side, marked off by an arcade of pointed and moulded arches with hexagonal columns and clerestory windows overhead (Fig. 104). The elaborate Gothic Revival main altar is set in front of the arched altar window with its intricate tracery. Here the original glazing was replaced in 1968 by the outstanding stained-glass work of George Walsh (Fig. 105).

Bottom left, opposite: Fig. 104—The plastered nave and side aisles of St Augustine's Church on Middle Street feature an arched arcade, pointed high-level windows, a wooden-framed roof and an elaborate Gothic Revival-style altar.

Bottom right, opposite: Fig. 105—The original glazing of the altar window of St Augustine's Church was replaced in 1968 by the magnificent stained-glass example created by George Walsh.

Above left: Fig. 102—The gabled entrance of St Augustine's Church on Middle Street stands on a raised stepped platform and features an arrangement of Gothic Revival features, including cut-stone work, buttresses and pointed-arched doors, as well as pointed and circular windows.

Above right: Fig. 103—The lean-to bay of St Augustine's Church on Middle Street has a strap-hinged sheeted door in a splayed and pointed archway, with a circular upper-level window immediately overhead.

41. Convent of Mercy church, Newtownsmith, 1840

The Sisters of Mercy arrived in Galway in 1840 and shortly afterwards laid out their convent, which included the Gothic Revival church, in Newtownsmith, on a site facing the River Corrib. Also known as Fr Daly's Chapel, after the notable Galway priest of the nineteenth century, the cut-stone building that faces the river has three gable-fronted bays, buttresses and a bell tower at one side. The triple-gabled front—similar to the triple elevation of St Nicholas's Collegiate Church (No. 1 above)—has a sequence of high-level pointed windows with hood-moulding, tracery and stained glass. The central window in particular is highly elaborate (Fig. 106). The building has an arched doorway at one end, but the door beside the bell tower was closed in the past and now acts as a window. The square bell tower is divided into three vertical stages with projecting string-courses, corner buttresses and a battlemented parapet (Fig. 107). The pointed tower doorway has projecting hood-mouldings with pointed overhead windows on the first-floor level. The upper section of the tower has a single pointed window with louvres. The interior of the church has a single nave with plastered walls and a ceiling decorated with moulded cornices, bosses and columns.

Fig. 106—The triple-gabled cut-stone Convent of Mercy church faces the River Corrib, its range of Gothic Revival elements including pointed-arched doors and windows, tracery and the corner bell tower.

Fig. 107—The bell tower of the Convent of Mercy church in Newtownsmith, when viewed from the nearby Salmon Weir Bridge, offers an imposing example of Gothic Revival ideals, including pointed arches, buttresses and rooftop battlements.

42. Former corner house, junction of Shop Street and Churchyard Street, 1890

The former house at the corner of Shop Street and Churchyard Street dates from 1890 and displays the typical features of a Victorian building. According, however, to the stone memorial plaque high up on the ground-level elevation on Shop Street it dates from 1562 (Fig. 108). This indicates that the present building has been superimposed onto a much earlier structure. The barely visible rectangular memorial stone carries the coats of arms of Thomas Martin and Elizabeth Lynch and a date of 1562. The rendered building now consists of a three-storey structure, with a prominent attic gable window, set into an irregular wedge-shaped plot (Fig. 109). The lined and rendered ground level has a glazed entrance door at the splayed apex of the block, as well as three large display windows facing Shop Street, above which the moulded fascia continues across the front. Overhead the Georgian-proportioned replacement sliding windows have moulded surrounds and keystones. At roof level the ornate dormer attic window is one of the most significant visual features of the building (Fig. 110). This is positioned on the apex of the hipped slated roof and acts as a visual focus from the central axis of the Shop Street approach. Today the building is in retail use on the ground floor and in commercial use overhead. The medieval plaque on the wall is barely noticeable owing to its size, in contrast to the surviving medieval arched doorway of a similar date on a house on the nearby High Street (Fig. 111), although the building itself, like the corner house, was replaced during the nineteenth century.

Fig. 108—Wall plaque over the shop fascia of the former corner house on Shop Street, with the coats of arms of Thomas Martin and Elizabeth Lynch and the date of 1562.

Fig. 109—The three-storey wedge-shaped former house at the apex of the junction of Shop Street and Churchyard Street has an arrangement of shop display windows, vertically proportioned upper-level windows and a distinctive attic dormer window at the apex of the block.

Fig. 110—The distinctive attic dormer window of the former house on Shop Street has a panelled face, camber-headed window, wedge-shaped arch stones, and a moulded triangular pediment that offers a prominent focal point from the Shop Street approach.

Fig. 111—The arched doorway on nearby High Street, adjacent to the former corner house on Shop Street, is the surviving remnant of a medieval building.

43. Corner retail store, William Street/Abbeygate Street, 1679–1890

The three-storey corner retail store at the junction of William Street and Abbeygate Street has its origins in the seventeenth century but was rebuilt around 1890. The rendered elevation is ruled, lined and scribed in imitation stonework and faces onto both streets, with a splayed bay at the corner (Fig. 112). The William Street elevation has a double entrance door with splayed side panels and a full-height display window set between narrow columns. The splay has a single display window, next to which the Abbeygate Street elevation has three display windows and a panelled end door. The elaborate overhead moulded fascia extends over the continuous shop fronts, with projecting curved brackets arranged over each of the ground-floor columns. The upper first- and second-floor levels have a range of uniformly spaced camber-headed windows with sliding sashes, above which the parapet has a continuous decorated moulding. The outstanding visual features of the building, however, are the stone memorial plaques on the upper-floor elevations. These include the 1679 date-stone and the Blake and Lynch coats of arms on the splay elevation (Fig. 113), and uncertain and Blake coats of arms on the William Street elevation (Fig. 114). The Abbeygate Street elevation also features a triangular panel built into the walling directly underneath the parapet decoration. The immediately adjoining premises on William Street also features several wall-mounted memorials.

Fig. 112—The rendered three-storey retail store on the corner of William Street and Abbeygate Street has a wrap-around shopfront and cambered upper-floor windows on both streets.

Fig. 113–The Blake and Lynch family coats of arms on the splay of the retail store at the William Street and Abbeygate Street intersection.

Fig. 114—Uncertain and Blake coats of arms on the William Street elevation of the corner retail store.

44. Office building, Merchant's Road, 1942

The office building on Merchant's Road is an interesting example of Art Deco—an early twentieth-century style characterised by plain geometric forms, plain rendered elevations and minimalist decoration. The symmetrical three-storey rendered building, which dates from 1942, has a slightly projecting central bay, flanked on either side by a narrower bay, and a high flat parapet that screens the roof behind (Fig. 115). The central bay has four tall, slim, sliding sash timber windows, grouped closely together and separated by slim rendered mullions, with the entrance porch slotted into the lower section. The porch is recessed, with a plain surround and a projecting canopy. The canopy has rounded corners, the edges decorated with shallow vertical ribs. The porch has a wooden sheeted outer double door and a glazed inner double door, incorporating vertical and horizontal glazing bars arranged in a typical Art Deco squared arrangement (Fig. 116). The central bay has a moulding of small square panels directly beneath the parapet coping. The side bays are slightly lower than the central bay, lack the parapet moulding and have three tall sash windows grouped closely together, similar to the central bay's window arrangement.

Above: Fig. 115—The distinctive three-storey Art Deco office building on Merchant's Road has three bays and a series of vertically proportioned windows.

Below: Fig. 116—The doorway of the Art Deco office building on Merchant's Road has glazed double doors and a curved canopy.

45. Galway Cathedral, University Road, 1965

Although built in 1965, well beyond the Victorian era, the architecture of the Catholic Cathedral of Our Lady Assumed into Heaven and St Nicholas reflects the Victorian approach to the use of past historical styles. The cathedral was laid out on the site of the former city gaol on the far side of the River Corrib and was designed by the architect John J. Robinson, with its side transept aligned on the central axis of the Salmon Weir Bridge to act as a counterpoint to the former courthouse (No. 22 above) on the far side of the bridge (Fig. 117). Today, with its copper roof, imposing scale and landscape foreground of the Corrib riverbank, it represents one of the major architectural set pieces of Galway city (Fig. 118). The cruciform-plan building follows no definitive architectural style but incorporates a number of historical architectural features, including rough-faced medieval-style masonry, square corner bell towers with turrets, round-headed windows and a tall copper-faced dome. This rises on

Fig. 117—Galway Cathedral on University Road was aligned on the central axis of the nineteenth-century Salmon Weir Bridge, with the mature landscape of the riverbank acting as a foreground.

Fig. 118—Galway Cathedral was arranged in a cruciform plan that incorporates a mixed range of historical elements, including rough-faced masonry, elaborate windows, dual bell towers and a dome.

a stone octagonal drum with triple round-headed windows, corner finials and the octagonal dome (Fig. 119). The other significant features of the elevation are the doors and windows. The north door has triple round-headed doors, side columns and carved semicircular overhead panels. The transept doorways have tall, glazed doors, slim cambered pediments and overhead rose-style windows. The tall, slim windows of the nave and transepts have round heads, while the large rose-shaped windows on the upper levels of the gables feature radial tracery. Internally the nave and transepts are separated from the lower side aisles by an arcade of columns and arches with rough stonework overhead (Fig. 120). The high- and low-level windows have decorated stained glass, and the barrel-vaulted ceiling has carved wooden panels. The outstanding internal feature is, however, the underside of the dome at the crossing of the nave and transepts, carried on decorated cross-vaults. This incorporates rough-faced stonework, an arcade of blind arches, an arrangement of triple round-headed windows and a plain curved centrepiece (Fig. 121).

Above left: Fig. 119—The copper dome of Galway Cathedral sits on an octagonal base with cross finials and is visible from many points across the city.

Above right: Fig. 120—The internal nave and transepts of Galway Cathedral are separated from the side aisles by an arcade of round-headed arches and rough stonework.

Fig. 121—The interior of the dome of Galway Cathedral, at the crossing of the nave and the transepts, is carried on decorated cross-vaults, above which there is an arcade of blind arches, an arrangement of triple round-headed windows and a plain curved centrepiece.